ENDORSEMENT

My introduction to Janet was when she contacted me in 2014 about the possibility of coming to spend some time with me as a student. Janet took the skills and the knowledge that she acquired and expanded them through patience, perseverance, and practice fueled by a love for the craft and especially her love of horses. Both passions are also reflected in *Braiding Horsehair Bracelets: Your Beginner's Guide.*

Anyone and everyone interested in learning the craft of horsehair braiding will benefit from this book which fills the current need for a more comprehensive and detailed tutorial. The colored photographs that accompany the written instructions will appeal to all readers, especially those who are visual learners.

Donna M. Murray
Lethbridge, Alberta, Canada
Custom Horsehair and Wool Creations
Winner of the Will Rogers Award for Horsehair Hitcher of the Year 2018, Academy of Western Artists (AWA)

BRAIDING HORSEHAIR BRACELETS

YOUR BEGINNER'S GUIDE

JANET WOLANIN ALEXANDER

CONTENTS

LIST OF ILLUSTRATIONS

ACKNOWLEDGEMENTS

To my husband Jim Alexander for his understanding, encouragement, and support during the long gestation of this book.

To Annette Farr and Donna Murray, my horsehair braiding teachers.

To Christopher Schilb for his computer support.

To Lesley A.J. Baumann, cover designer.

To Letha Cupp for the photographs she contributed.

To Sandra Duclos and Donna Cowan, editorial consultants.

To Mary Wolanin and Jim Alexander for their proofreading assistance.

To my Swishtails Custom Horsehair Jewelry customers.

To the Indiana Arts Commission for my 2014 Individual Artist Program Grant.

To the Circle C Ranch (Borden, IN) for Alabama's black and white tail hair.

Thank you for your help in birthing this book!

INTRODUCTION

Some people love horses while others love crafts. Having picked up this book, you might love both. Or perhaps you are a craftsperson who wants to surprise a horse-crazy friend or relative with a bracelet made from the hair of a special horse. Whatever your motivation and whether you recently discovered horsehair jewelry or have known about it for a while, if you want to begin learning how to braid, welcome!

This book is for you. I wrote it to share my love of working with horsehair, and to save you some of the time and frustration that I went through during my quest to learn how to braid it into jewelry.

I find horsehair tactilely pleasant to work with. It is so beautiful—in the light, it resembles flexible strands of cool spun glass. And it is endlessly fascinating. For example, did you know that the tails of all chestnut horses are not solid red? My horse's body and mane are red, but his tail is red, black, and white, often with two or three colors in a single strand and sometimes in a repeating pattern! While his tail hair appears red when worn loose in the sun, it is brownish tweed when compressed into a braid.

Just to be clear, this book is not one that teaches how to braid manes and tails for horse shows, but rather one that introduces how to braid legally harvested tail hair into jewelry. Mane hair is usually too short and too fine for jewelry braiding.

Braiding horsehair requires more preparation and instruction than plaiting human hair into the standard 3-string braid. Introductory steps are available here and there in books, magazines, and on the Internet, but I do not know of a comprehensive instruction guide that has compiled all of them together. The main purpose of this book is to fill that void. It will teach you how to turn a bit of horsehair into a piece of jewelry you can proudly wear. Join the fiber artists around the world who, throughout human history, have fashioned practical and decorative items from this renewable and natural resource.

As a retired teacher, I know that people learn differently. I cannot easily decipher written instructions or black and white illustrations and learn crafts best hands-on and one-on-one. This is why I dedicated so much time searching for my horsehair teachers. Because they were hard to find and I cannot personally pass down what they taught me to many people, hopefully writing out and photographing the steps will help many readers.

Learning to create the three basic bracelets in this book—the 4-string round braid, the 6-string half-round braid, and a simple version of an 8-string round braid—might satisfy you. And if you wish to further your skills, you will have a solid foundation. But should you discover that braiding horsehair jewelry is not the craft for you—it requires good close-up vision, attention to detail, fine motor skills, patience, and lots of practice—no worries. You can buy horsehair jewelry from artists who braid and sell a dazzling array and you will better appreciate their work having first tried your own hand at the craft.

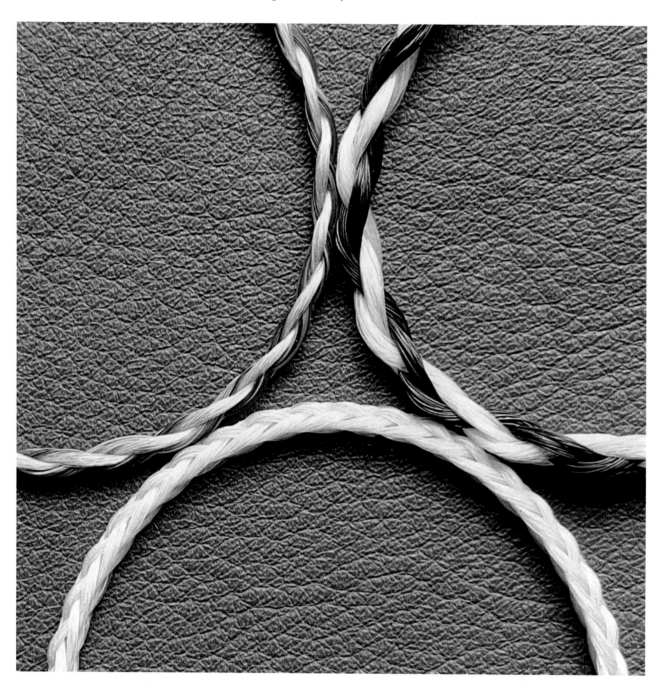

Figure I.1: Clockwise from the top left: a red and white 4-string round braid in the striped pattern, a black and white easy 8-string round braid in the spiral pattern, and a 6-string half-round braid in cream.

CHAPTER ONE
OBTAINING A HORSE'S TAIL HAIR

Before I begin, please know that all the steps in this book are presented the way I do them which are my take on what I was taught. As you gain experience, you will probably make your own adaptations.

Ready? Let us start!

HARVESTING VS. PURCHASING

There are two ways of obtaining horsehair: you can purchase it or you can harvest it. (Harvesting means cutting off what you need in an unnoticeable way.) Consider your situation in deciding which option is better for you.

The Purchase Option. Unless you are horse savvy and have access to a safe horse, I suggest that you buy your tail hair from a legal business. This option will cost money but allow you to select from assorted colors, and because the hair will probably arrive pre-washed, combed, and of equal length, it will save you preparation time.

I hate to tell you this, but you need to know that horsehair pirates exist. They have been known to cut off the entire tails of horses to make a quick, illegal buck. This is not only stealing, it is cruelty because horses need their tails to swish off insects that bite, sting, and lay parasite eggs, thus potentially introducing diseases into their bodies. It is important that you buy your hair from a credible established business.

If you opt to purchase horsehair, your first assignment is to start researching legitimate businesses that sell it and decide how much and which color(s) and length(s) you wish to buy. Horsehair is typically sold by the pound. Rare colors are more expensive than common ones. I suggest selecting the smallest bundle of tail hair available between 18-24 inches long. The bundle should contain more than enough hair for the bracelets in this book; the excess will come in handy for practicing the braids and for future projects. If your pocketbook allows, you might also buy a second color of tail hair. Two contrasting hues will allow you to learn some color patterns in addition to the braiding patterns.

When your hair arrives you can skip reading the rest of this chapter and advance to Chapter Two.

The Harvesting Option. If you own a horse or know a willing horse owner, you might choose harvesting just the amount of tail hair needed for the 4-string round braid, your first assignment.

Your investment will be the time and labor involved in harvesting the hair as well as preparing it for braiding. Your chief advantage? A bracelet braided from the tail hair of a beloved horse has much more emotional significance than one braided from that of an unknown horse. Many an owner honors a special horse by, during its lifetime or upon its passing, harvesting some hair for the creation of a keepsake.

Once you harvest your hair—again, one color is enough for this book, but two colors will give you the opportunity to learn a few color patterns—please complete all the directions in this chapter before moving on to the next.

MATERIALS

a wide-toothed horse comb, curry, or fairly stiff horse brush
a pair of medium, blunt-tipped scissors
a clear, large, self-locking plastic bag
a permanent marker
a few rubber bands
optional: an equine detangler

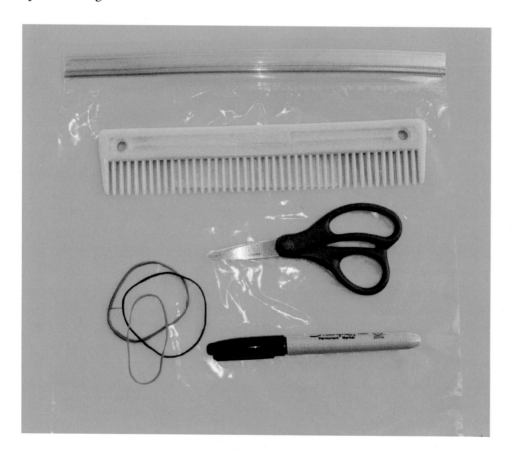

Figure 1.1: Materials needed.

HOW TO HARVEST TAIL HAIR

Alabama, a gelding at my horse's stable, will serve as your model. I chose him because of his good nature and bi-color tail.

1. Secure the horse. Someone can hold its halter or you can cross-tie or slip-tie it to a hitching post.

2. Approach the horse from the side so it can see you. Introduce yourself by talking to it soothingly and stroking it gently. Slowly make your way to its hind end but do not stand directly behind it.

Figure 1.2: Stand next to the horse or at an angle behind it.

3. Brush the mud, hay, stickers, burrs, etc. from its tail. If the hair is tangled, work some detangler through it.

4. Write the horse's name on the plastic bag with permanent marker.

5. Locate the horse's dock, the bone extending from its spine (Figure 1.3). Soft skin (pink on Alabama) covers the muscles surrounding the bone from which the hair extends, except on the underside.

Figure 1.3: The dock.

6. Carefully raise the tail to parallel with the ground and notice if any "icicles" (naturally formed sections of hair) dangle down (Figure 1.4). For your first bracelet, the 4-string round, select two sections of hair each about as wide in diameter as a pencil. To avoid creating a large bare spot, cut each section from a different place. For my 4-string demonstration braid, I cut one section of black hair and one of white hair.

Figure 1.4: Hanging "icicles" (sections of hair).

7. To protect the horse's dock from accidental puncture and bleeding, pinch each selected "icicle" between two fingers of your non-dominant hand at its attachment to the dock (Figure 1.5). Then, with your dominant hand, cut the section off above those fingers.

Figure 1.5: Cutting off an "icicle."

8. Rubber-band the cut section of hair at its thicker (upper or body end) before any hairs slip out-of-place. If you are braiding your 4-string bracelet from one color of hair, you will need to cut a second "icicle" of the same color. Remove the rubber band from the first cut, align its top with that of the second, band the two cuts together, coil the new bundle, and slip it into your bag.

   If, however, you are braiding your bracelet from two colors, your second cut might be of a contrasting color. Once this cut is rubber-banded (separately from your first color) and coiled, you can slip it into the same bag. Secure the bag, so you don't lose any of your hard-earned treasure.

   Don't worry if you are collecting tail hair from two special horses whose tails do not contrast much in color. Honoring them is much more important than how much their tails contrast. I once made a bracelet with red hair and gray hair and it turned out just fine, the pattern was just subtler. If the two colors are even more similar, you can create a tweed braid by making pulls from half of one horse's hairs and half from the other's.

9. Gather your supplies, thank the horse and its owner, and return the horse to its stall or pasture.

   Suggestion: An on-line video may help you to better visualize the harvesting process.

CHAPTER TWO
PREPARING TAIL HAIR FOR BRAIDING

To protect your horsehair, the steps in this chapter are best done in pet-free zones. My cats and dogs like to steal, tangle, chew, and even swallow horsehair. To prevent them from developing intestinal blockages, I try to keep them out of my work zone.

<u>Materials</u>

shampoo (If you do not own horse shampoo, use your own hair brand.)
a plastic pocket comb like the one in Figure 2.1
hand, baby, or wet wipes
horsehair

- 4-string bracelet: 2 pencil width bundles of one color or one each of two colors

- 8-string bracelet: 4 pencil width bundles of one color or two each of two colors

- 6-string bracelet: 3 pencil width bundles of one color, or one of one color and two of a second color

Figure 2.1: A plastic pocket comb with two different sizes of teeth.

Steps

1. Rinse or shampoo the hair.

    A. Purchased hair. If your hair looks clean, make sure that it is either rubber-banded at the thick end or loosely tied intermittently along its length with cotton string. Thoroughly rinse the bundle with water to remove any chemicals or pesticides that may have been applied during shipping. If you are working with two or more colors of hair, keep each bundle separate.

    B. Harvested hair. Shampoo and rinse the bundle(s) until the hair looks clean and the water runs clear. You can carefully shimmy the rubber band(s) down the bundle(s) and wash underneath.

    A and B. Let the hair air dry. In warm weather, I hang the bundles where animals cannot get to them. During the rest of the year, I lay them on a clean towel in a closed room.

2. Comb the hair.

    A. Purchased hair. Combing is not necessary for hair that comes pre-combed, cleaned, bundled, and cut to the same length. Simply remove the required pencil-widths of hair (remember, two for the 4-string bracelet, four for the 8-string bracelet, and three for the 6-string bracelet), combine and rubber-band the pencil-widths at the thicker end, and advance to Step 3.

    B. Harvested hair. Because this step can get messy, it is best done outdoors. Indoors, it is best done over a garbage can or newspaper for easy cleanup.

The purpose of this step is to remove most of the hairs that are too short for your bracelet. Many of them broke when the horse rubbed its tail (e.g., against a fence post or a tree trunk) or pasture mates chewed them. The hair at the bottom of your bundle will probably be layered rather than bluntly cut, and the hair at the top will be thicker than that at the bottom. Because there is more short hair at the top, I prefer to comb the top half first.

Firmly grasp your bundle of hair in the middle with your non-dominant hand and carefully remove the rubber band with your dominant hand. Keep it close for re-use. With your dominant hand, gently comb the hair from the middle of the bundle to the top end (Figure 2.2). When the comb glides through easily in this direction, flip the bundle 180 degrees and comb out the short hairs on the opposite end.

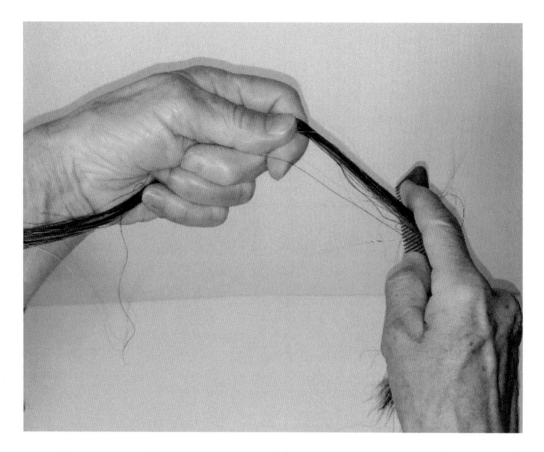

Figure 2.2: Combing a pencil-width bundle of hair to remove the short pieces.

When you are through, re-band your hair at the top of the thicker end, still securely, but a little looser than before.

Special note about white hair yellowed at the bottom and black hair sunburned red at the bottom: if the hair is significantly longer than your intended bracelet, you can trim off some of the excess yellow or red hair before proceeding to Step 3.

3. Make eight pulls.

   Pulls are the number of hairs you need to remove from a bundle of horsehair, inspect for length, and knot together at one end. You want to avoid braiding with short hairs that will stick out and affect both your bracelet's appearance and its comfort. Two pulls twisted together create one string.

   I recommend between 8-10 hairs per pull: 8 for coarse hair, 9 for medium-textured hair, and 10 for fine hair. The reason? Your braid needs to fit into your end caps, and when you plait hair from two (or more) horses that differs in texture, their string circumferences should match.

   A. To make a pull, hold your bundle of hair with your non-dominant hand. With your dominant hand, pinch and try to pull out the number of hairs you need from the bottom end (Figure 2.3). If you are working with untrimmed, harvested hair, you can either start pulling out the longest hairs first or evenly trim the bottom of an uneven bundle before starting your pulls.

Figure 2.3: Pulling hair from a bundle to make a pull.

If you are lucky, you will pull out the exact number of hairs you need, but most likely you will need to either pinch out a few more or eliminate a few to attain your goal.

B. Once you have the needed number of hairs in your pull, remove half, and flip their direction. Then recombine, align, and tightly knot all the hairs together at one end. This ensures the creation of a braid with a consistent width instead of a tapering (carrot-shaped) one.

C. Repeat Steps 3A and 3B seven more times. Then tighten the band or string around your remaining hair. Keep the extra hair nearby while you braid—if hairs slip out of their pulls or break during preparation, you will need replacements.

4. Wipe the hair.

As far as I know, I invented this step upon noticing that hairs that look clean (especially black ones) can still be dirty.

Side story: One spring, a client ordered a bracelet for her daughter's Easter basket while another woman, upon seeing the picture of a braided bracelet on my business card, burst out with, "Gross, who wants to wear jewelry with dried horse poo on it?!" Go figure!

More commonly, people with allergies to cats and dogs wonder if they are also allergic to horsehair. Of course, they will not know until they wear it, but you should do your best to braid with clean hair. I clean horsehair twice before braiding and once afterward (as you will learn in Chapter Seven). Also, once you get good at braiding bracelets, you can upgrade from inexpensive metal findings to hypoallergenic ones (e.g. sterling silver) to reduce the potential of a metal allergy.

Back to wiping…gently fold a wet wipe around a pull at the knotted end. Holding the knot firmly with your non-dominant hand, firmly pull the wipe all the way down the braid (upwards in Figure 2.4) with your dominant hand. If the hair leaves a dirty streak on the wet wipe, re-swipe in a clean spot. Repeat until the wipe comes out clean.

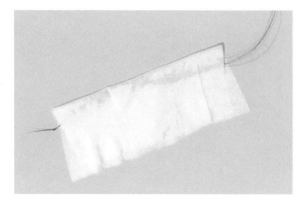

Figure 2.4: Wet-wiping a pull.

Warning: Avoid using dry paper wipes, especially on black hair. They create fuzz that is very hard to remove.

5. In this step you will twist pairs of pulls into strings. Twists are key to creating attractive, comfortable bracelets. Twisting is awkward at first and takes a lot of practice to execute well, so do not be discouraged. Before you start, read the rest of the directions in this step carefully to visualize the entire process.

    A. Pick up two pulls and tie them together just below their individual knots. Insert the forefinger of your dominant hand under the knot between the two pulls (Figure 2.5). Use your thumb and middle finger to catch and press each pull against your index finger.

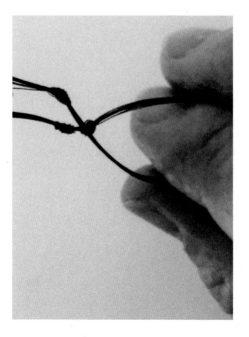

Figure 2.5: Preparing to twist two pulls.

B. Pinch the new knot between the thumb and forefinger of your non-dominant hand and start rotating it (Figure 2.6). As your twist grows in length, slide your dominant thumb, index finger, and middle finger down the pulls.

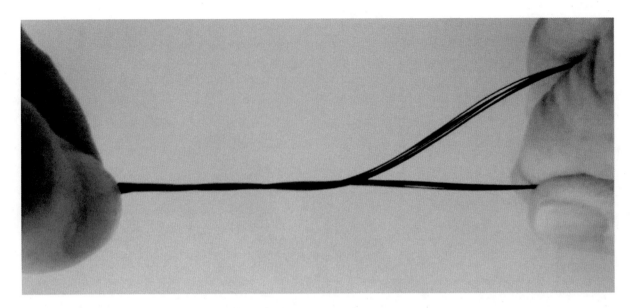

Figure 2.6: Twisting two pulls.

Be sure to keep the untwisted hairs in the two pulls beneath your right hand completely separate until it is time to twist them—you want to avoid a tangle. I like to sit with a pull draped over each side of my thigh. Twist almost down to the shortest hair of an uneven pull or at least an inch above the bottom of an even pull.

C. Then knot the two twisted pulls together at the bottom. Ta-da! You just made your first string!

Figure 2.7: A completed string. Which end is the start and which is the end?

The key to making a good string is applying and maintaining even pressure as you twist pairs of pulls. I have heard that some braiders hold the top knot in their mouths while twisting their pulls—another reason for clean hair—but I have not observed anyone doing so.

When you release a completed string, your two pulls should stay twisted and no hairs should arc or poke out. This may seem impossible upon your first try, but it is possible. Just keep practicing.

If a twist unravels after you knot it at the bottom, try unknotting the bottom knot, separating the two pulls up to the top knot, re-twisting them, and re-knotting them at the bottom. If you are unsuccessful, toss the twist and start over with a new set of pulls.

Good strings make good braids.

CHAPTER THREE
LEARNING THE 4-STRING ROUND BRAIDING PATTERN, U2O1 (OR O2U1)

When I first heard the term 4-string braid, I literally pictured a very thin bracelet plaited from four hairs—which, of course, made no sense! So let us take a moment to review some vocabulary and recap your accomplishments in the previous chapter.

In Chapter Two you selected the number of *strands* of horsehair (i.e., individual hairs) needed to make eight *pulls*. After flipping half of the hairs in each pull in the opposite direction, you realigned all the hairs at one end and knotted them. Next, you twisted pairs of pulls together to make *strings*.

More than one braiding pattern can be made with the same number of strings. Thus, there are many 4-, 6-, and 8-string braiding patterns. For clarity, I refer to the braids in this book as the 4-string round, the 6-string half-round (picture a loaf of bread or the shape of a capital D), and the 8-string easy-round.

<u>Materials</u>: Figure 3.1

the 4 horsehair strings you made in Chapter Two
four 3-foot lengths of parachute cord* (four of one color, or two each of two colors)
a retractable cloth measuring tape marked into millimeter (mm) and ⅛" (inch) increments
a 12" ruler marked into millimeter and ⅛" increments
scissors
an S-hook
a few inches of cotton string
some 1 mm wide waxed cotton cord
at least two twist ties
1-2 rectangular, flat barrettes
optional: a lighter or matches to singe the ends of the parachute cords to prevent unraveling

* Parachute cord is sized according to its tensile (minimal breaking) strength which ranges from micro to 750# (pounds). In this book, both the traditional #550 size and the slightly thinner #325 size have been used. Either size is recommended.

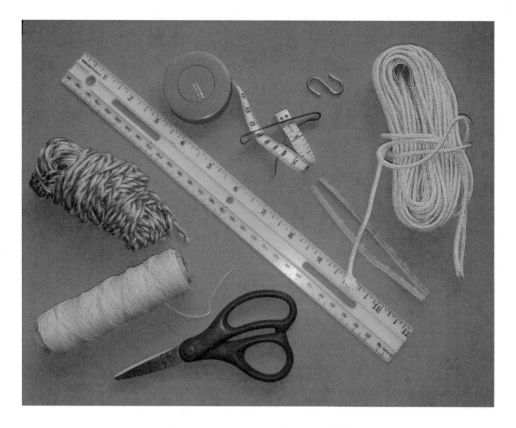

Figure 3.1: Materials needed.

The rest of this chapter divides into two parts: learning the 4-string round braiding pattern and your fingering with parachute cord, and then repeating this skill with your thinner, slicker, and less cooperative horsehair strings. Remember, you first learned to color with fat crayons, write with fat pencils, and paint with fat brushes before graduating to thinner ones.

BRAIDING WITH PARACHUTE CORD

Instructions are written for right-handed readers with occasional notes to left-handed ones.

1. Set up your work site.

    The beauty of horsehair braiding is that it can be done almost anywhere with very few and inexpensive tools. You can braid outdoors from a base such as a nail on a fence or indoors from the leg of a table or the rung of a chair. You can braid standing or seated on the floor or at a table with a C-clamp or small hobby vise attached to it. (See Figure 9.1.) I like to sit on a wheeled office chair, affix my horsehair to a handle on my metal file cabinet, and scoot back as I braid.

    Begin by tightly tying a short loop of cotton string around your base. Hang one end of the S-hook on the loop.

2. Lay out your four parachute cords from left to right in one of these color patterns: AABB (e.g., two green and two pink cords), ABAB (e.g., a green cord, a pink cord, a green cord, and a pink cord), or AAAA (e.g., four green cords).

Align your four lengths of parachute cord together at one end and tightly knot them. Below the knot, tightly tie a piece of thin cord around the parachute cords. Knot the two loose ends of the thin cord to form a loop. Hang the loop on the empty end of the S-hook. Make sure all your knots are tight because you will pull against them as you braid.

Realign the parachute cords into your color pattern, slip a barrette across them, and snug it up underneath the parachute cord knot to hold the cords flat and in order. (Figure 3.2).

Figure 3.2: Setting up a 4-string round braid with two colors of parachute cord.

The cord on the far right is in Position 1; the cord to its left is in Position 2; the cord to its left is in Position 3; and the cord on the far left is in Position 4. As you braid, your cords will change positions but the positions will retain the same numbers.

3. Before braiding the cords, read and visualize the rest of this step. It uses four different colors of cord to depict the 4-string round braid.

Memorize the pattern for the 4-string round braid: under two cords and back over one cord. It is abbreviated U2O1 (U=under, O=over). The inverse, O2U1, works too.

Chanting a mantra while braiding may prevent you from daydreaming and losing your place. I suggest: "right under two, back over one, and tighten; left under two, back over one, and tighten."

Starting position: four different colors of parachute cord are knotted and arranged from left to right. A barrette is placed around the cords and then snugged up under the top knot to hold the cords flat and in order (Figure 3.3).

Figure 3.3: Setting up the 4-strand round braid with four colors of parachute cord.

Now, imagine yourself:

- pinching strings 2 and 1 between your right thumb and first two fingers, and strings 4 and 3 between your left thumb and first two fingers.

- starting on the right side, picking up the green cord in Position 1 and passing it under the cords in Positions 2 and 3 and then back over the cord to the right.

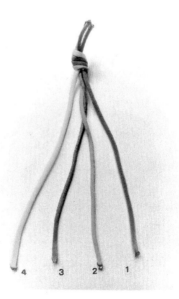

Figure 3.4: Result of right (green) under two, over one.

Next, imagine picking up the yellow cord in Position 4 and placing it under the cords in Positions 3 and 2 and then back over the cord to the left.

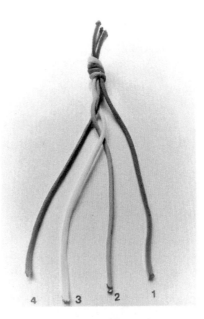

Figure 3.5: Result of left (yellow) under two, over one.

Envision yourself doing two more steps.

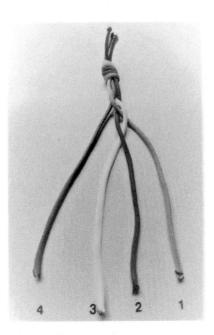

Figure 3.6: Result of right (pink) under two, over one and...

Figure 3.7: …left (blue) under two, over one.

Notice that your cords are now back in their starting positions—from positions 4-1 (or left to right): yellow, blue, pink, and green. Because this is a 4-string braid, it takes four steps to complete a braiding sequence.

Continue braiding.

Figure 3.8: The result of four sequences of braiding with four colors of parachute cord.

Observe that the color pattern at the end of the braid in Figure 3.8 is a repeat of the ending pattern in Figures 3.3 and 3.7. Also notice my use of the barrette in securing the end of the braid in Figure 3.8 before taking the photo. Scan the braid between the top knot and the barrette. Do you see four "stitches" of each color?

18

A just-for-fun discovery: to prove that strings need to be longer than the length of a desired braid, the four 12" cords in Step 3 yielded the 4" braid in Figure 3.8.

4. Tag, you are it! Go back to the parachute braid you set up in Step 2 and start practicing your braiding moves. When you start, you will notice that the loose ends of the hanging cords will tend to tangle as you braid. To prevent knotting, frequently comb through them with your fingers.

    After you are through with your first parachute braid, save it. Resume braiding with fresh cord and reuse those cords over and over. By comparing your first braid to your future ones, you can observe your improvement.

    Once you have mastered the 4-string round pattern, start concentrating on making tight, even braids. The secret is to consistently pull each pair of strings after placing them in their new positions.

    What kind of pattern did you create with the color pattern you chose in Step 3? One of my very favorite things about braiding is experimenting with different color patterns. Rearranging the strings into different color patterns between practice rounds is enjoyable as well as educational. But braiding the same color pattern over and over is very meditative. Either way, you cannot lose!

BRAIDING WITH HORSEHAIR

Once you are adept in braiding the 4-string round pattern with parachute cord, it is time to advance to braiding with horsehair—which, unlike parachute cord, is thinner and less cooperative, often, like a horse, seeming to have a mind of its own!

One last thing, it does not matter which way you line up your strings before braiding—with all the single knots at the top, all the double knots at the top, or a combination thereof.

Figure 3.9: Starting a 4-string round braid with horsehair.

Stop braiding harvested hair with uneven bottom lengths above the shortest hair to prevent it from sticking out of your braid. You can braid purchased hair of even bottom lengths until your grip starts to feel tenuous.

Practice braiding your 4-string horsehair braid over and over, applying even tension from beginning to end, until your fingers develop muscle memory. Again, you may wish to tie off and save your first horsehair braid as a "measuring stick" from which to observe your improvement.

When you are satisfied with a braid and ready to turn it into a bracelet, tightly twist-tie the top of the braid at the point where it becomes consistently round. Twist-tie the braid at the bottom too. (See Figure 3.10.)

Figure 3.10: Ending a 4-string round horsehair braid.

Remove your braid from the S-hook and the barrette (if you used one) from the braid. Visually inspect the braid. Run your fingers down it. Do you feel any irregularities? Finally, lay it on the table and observe how well it holds together on its own.

If you observe a braiding error and are up for the challenge, instead of unbraiding the entire braid and starting over, try slowly unbraiding backward step-by-step to the step above the error and re-braiding from there.

However, if your braid looks and feels error-free, pat yourself on the back and advance to Chapters 5 and 6 to learn about findings and how to apply them.

CHAPTER FOUR

LEARNING THE EASY 8-STRING ROUND PATTERN, U2O1 (OR O2U1)

Materials. The same as Chapter Three, except with eight pieces of parachute cord and eight strings of horsehair instead of four. All eight can be the same color, or four can be one color and four a second contrasting color.

BRAIDING WITH PARACHUTE CORD

1. Set up your work site.

2. Arrange the eight parachute cords from left to right in one of these color patterns: AAAAAAAA (e.g., eight green cords) or AABBAABB (e.g., two green cords, two pink cords, two green cords, and two pink cords). Knot them together at the top. If you wish, slip a barrette beneath the parachute cord knot to hold your arrangement in place. Snug it up beneath the knot.

Figure 4.1: Setting up an 8-eight string easy-round braid with two colors of parachute cord.

The first set of pink cords on the far right is in Position 1; the first green set to its left is in Position 2; the next set of pink cords is in Position 3; and the second set of green cords on the far left is in Position 4. As you braid, your cords will change positions but the positions will retain their same numbers.

3. The pattern for the easy 8-string round braid is the same as the pattern for the 4-string round braid with one exception—the strings are braided in pairs instead of individually. In this case, U2O1 means that the pair of strings on the right are placed under two pairs of strings on the left and then back over one pair, followed by placement of the pair of strings on the left under two pairs and back over one. Again, the inverse of U2O1 is O2U1.

    Part your cords in half, those in positions 1-4 to the right and those in positions 5-8 to the left. The space between them should resemble an upside down V.

    Starting on the right side, pick up the cords in Positions 1&2 and place them under cords in Positions 3-6, and then back over the pair of cords to the right.

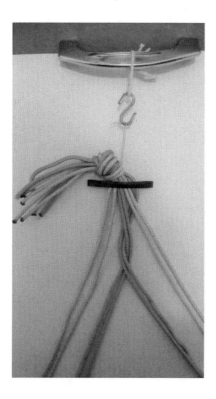

Figure 4.2: Result of right pair (pink) under two pairs and back over one pair.

Repeat the reverse of this step from the left side. Pick up the cords in Positions 7&8 and place them under the cords in Positions 6-3 and back over the pair of cords to the left. Divide the four cords in half again.

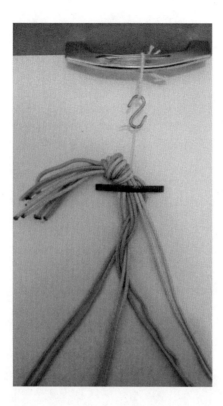

Figure 4.3: Result of left pair (green) under two pairs and back over one pair.

Repeat this set of steps to complete one sequence.

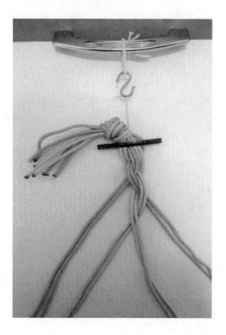

Figure 4.4: Result of right pair (green) under two pairs and back over one pair.

Figure 4.5: Result of left (pink) under two pairs and back over one pair.

Now that you have completed one complete sequence of braiding, you are back to the beginning color pattern (GGPPGGPP) and your braid is no longer flat. Keep braiding until you run low on cord.

Figures 4.6 and 4.7 show the braid after four sequences.

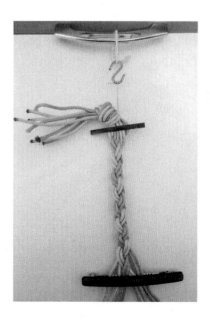

Figure 4.6: Four sequences with a top barrette.   Figure 4.7: Four sequences without a top barrette.

See all the wasted braid at the top of Figure 4.6? You will avoid this once you no longer rely on a top barrette to start your braid and can manage all your strings with your hands.

When you reach the end of your braid, inspect it for errors. You may wish to save your first braid for comparison to your future braids and continue practicing with eight new cords that you can braid and unbraid over and over, perhaps in different color patterns.

Practice until you consistently produce error-free braids with even tightness throughout.

BRAIDING WITH HORSEHAIR

Once you are confident in braiding the 8-string round pattern with parachute cord, try braiding it with horsehair.

Figure 4.8: Starting an easy 8-string round horsehair braid without a top barrette.

Figure 4.9: Ending an easy 8-string round horsehair braid.

Note the hairs bowing out from black string #4 below the barrette and from white strings #1,2, and 5 above it. Bowing and untwisting can occur after repeated hair handling. This braid is long enough to be knotted above all the bowing. The bowing beneath the knot will not matter as it will eventually be cut off. You will probably find, that no matter how good you get at twisting, some textures of hair are just harder to twist than others.

When you are ready to finish your horsehair bracelet, advance to Chapters 6 and 7 for instructions on metal findings and how to attach them. Whoo-hoo!

CHAPTER FIVE

LEARNING THE 6-STRING HALF-ROUND BRAIDING PATTERN, U4O2 (OR O4U2)

This braid is my favorite of the three taught in this book. It makes a bracelet that, having a flat side, lies flat against your wrist.

<u>Materials</u>. The same as in Chapter Three except with six lengths of parachute cord and horsehair strings instead of four. All six can be the same color, or four can be one color and two a second color.

BRAIDING WITH PARACHUTE CORD

1. Set up your work site.

2. Arrange the six parachute cords from left to right in one of these color patterns: AAAAAA (e.g., six green cords) or AABBAA (e.g., two green, two pink, and two green cords).

Figure 5.1: Setting up a 6-string half-round braid with two colors of parachute cord.

The strand on the far right is in Position 1; the string to its left is in Position 2; the one to its left is in Position 3; and so on. The cord on the far left is in Position 6. As you braid, your strings will change positions but the positions will retain their same numbers. Do you still need to use a barrette to start your braids?

3.   Before you begin, study the pattern braided with six colors of cord in Figures 5.2-5.10. You will start your own braid in Step 4.

The pattern for the 6-string half-round braid is under four cords and back over two cords. Its abbreviation is U4O2 (U=under, O=over) and the inverse, O4U2, works too.

Figure 5.2 shows the starting position of six colors of knotted parachute cord. Remember Roy G. Biv? To make the pattern easy to track, I chose rainbow-colored cords—minus indigo and with black instead of violet (out of stock at my craft store when I went shopping).

Figure 5.2: Setting up a 6-string half-round braid with six colors of parachute cord.

The r-ed cord is in 1st position, the o-range in 2nd, the y-ellow in 3rd, the g-reen in 4th, the b-lue in 5th, and the black (standing in for v-iolet) in 6th. The separation between the three strings on the left and the three strings on the right is necessary for holding and tightening after each step.

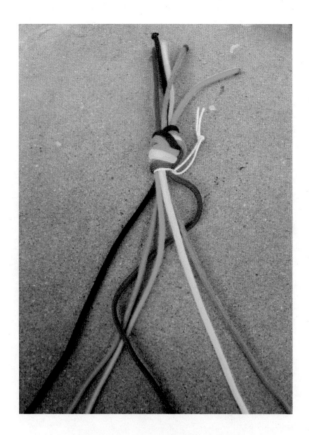

Figure 5.3: Right (red) U4O2.

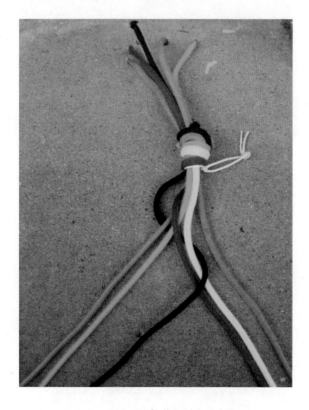

Figure 5.4: Left (black) U4O2.

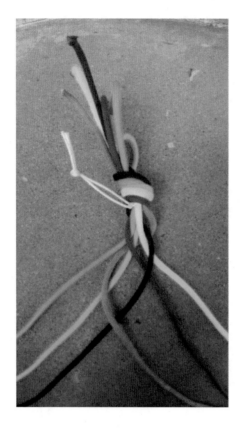

Figure 5.5: Right: (orange) U4O2.

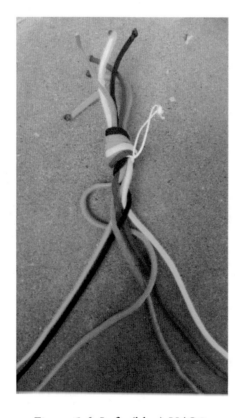

Figure 5.6: Left: (blue) U4O2.

Figure 5.7: Right: (yellow) U4O2.

Figure 5.8: Left: (green) U4O2.

Notice that one sequence of six steps has been completed and the six strings are back in their starting color order. Keep braiding.

When you are finished, observe that one side of the braid is flat whereas the opposite side is round, hence the name of the braid.

Figure 5.9: The flat side of the 6-string half-round braid.

Figure 5.10: The round side of the 6-string half-round braid.

4. Now go back to the parachute cords you set up in Step 2 and try out this new braiding pattern.

BRAIDING WITH HORSEHAIR

Repeat the 6-string half-round pattern with horsehair. Practice until you are happy with the outcome of a braid. Then twist-tie it off at both ends.

Figure 5.11: A completed 6-string half-round horsehair braid twist-tied off at both ends.

Remove your braid from the S-hook and inspect it for mistakes.

If there appear to be none, hurrah! It is time to apply the metal findings! See Chapters 6 and 7.

Chapter Six

Obtaining the Materials for Finishing Your Bracelet(s)

The purpose of this step is to obtain the findings (metal parts) and associated materials necessary for completing your horsehair bracelet.

Findings: end caps, clasps, and rings. I recommend buying ones made from inexpensive base metals (e.g., iron, nickel, copper, or brass) during the learning and practice stages. After you are proficient, you can graduate to silver-plated findings or ones made of more expensive metals (e.g., sterling silver). Shop for findings at local craft stores and on-line jewelry sites.

Findings come in a variety of prices, sizes, and designs. You want end caps, clasps, and rings that are proportional to each other and match the width of the braid they adorn. Below are my recommendations for starting out. Beware that shopping requires time, patience, and attention to detail.

1. End caps with crimps and attached loops. You need two such end caps per bracelet.

    Caps encase the ends of your braid. End caps with loops allow attachment to rings and clasps. I prefer end caps also designed to crimp (i.e., compress with pliers upon braids) to reinforce the gluing. End caps are sized according to the diameter of their barrels. ID refers to the size of the inner diameter; OD refers to the size of the outer diameter.

    End caps vary in size and tend to go in and out of style. Figure 6.1 contains the crimp styles available for the braids in this book upon publication. The crimp in the 4-string end cap is the bottom ring in the coil; the crimp in the 6- and the 8-string end caps is the middle of the three barrel "rolls."

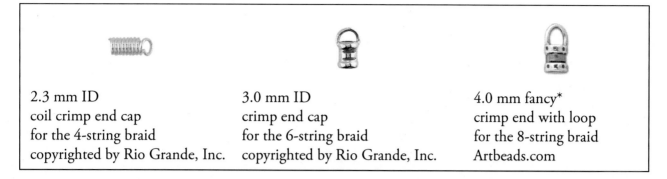

Figure 6.1: Crimp end caps.

* 3.8 mm three-part barrel crimp end caps also work for 8-string braids.

2. Clasps. You need one clasp per bracelet. Clasps also come in various styles and sizes. I recommend starting out with an oval lobster clasp for your 4-string round bracelet, and teardrop oval lobster clasps for your 6- and 8-string bracelets.

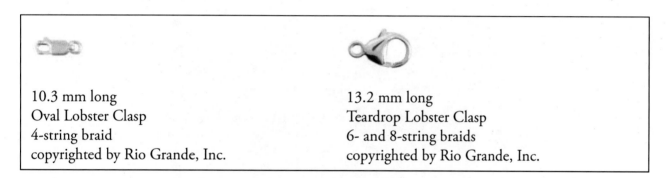

Figure 6.2: Lobster clasps.

3. Rings. You need either split rings or open jump rings. Both come in different sizes. It is a good idea to buy more than you need because they are easy to pull out of shape during the practice stage.

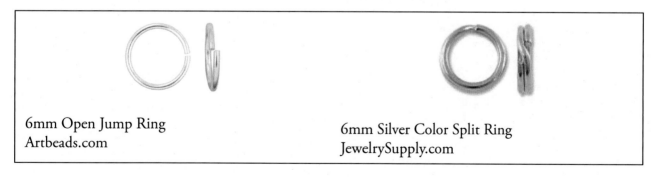

Figure 6.3: The open jump ring (left) vs the split ring (right).

An open jump ring has a cut that allows it to be opened, placed around the loop of an end cap or a clasp, and closed. Online videos teach the correct way to open and close jump rings. In Figure 6.3, the open jump ring's split is at the 3:00 position.

You can also see in Figure 6.3 that a split ring is a double-wrap of two tightly pressed coils resembling a tiny key chain. A special pair of pliers called a split ring jewelry opener helps you to open and attach these rings without breaking your fingernails.

Tools and Materials.

pair of sharp scissors
a foot-long ruler marked in inches and millimeters
a retracting cloth measuring tape marked in inches and millimeters
a few twist ties
a few wooden toothpicks
strong glue: Braiders vary in the types of glue they use. I use a brand of shoe cement.
pliers: Craft stores often carry jewelry pliers. I also like to use flat-nosed pliers.

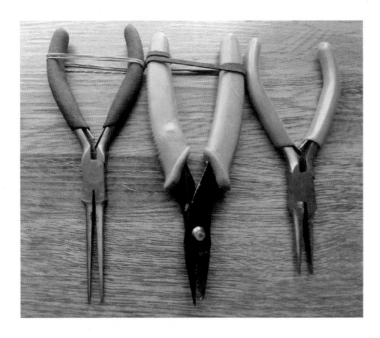

Figure 6.4: Pliers, from left to right—needle-nose, split ring jewelry opener, and chain-nose.

CHAPTER SEVEN
ASSEMBLING YOUR BRACELET(S)

Yay, the last step! This chapter includes many detailed instructions but a quality piece of jewelry will be your reward. Slow and steady is the way to go.

While findings are sized in the Metric System, the assembly steps are written in the American Measurement System.

1. <u>Measure the bracelet recipient's wrist</u>. Needed: a cloth measuring tape (because it flexes without stretching).

   Use your tape to measure the circumference of the wrist at the preferred place of wearing (e.g. high, low, or in between on the wrist) to the nearest ⅛ᵗʰ" (one-eighth of an inch). If you are making the bracelet for yourself and have difficulty measuring your own wrist, ask a friend or family member for help.

   Take the measurement three times to make sure it is correct. Proper fit is essential and you can usually only cut a braid once.

2. <u>Calculate the length of braid required for the bracelet</u>. Needed: findings, tools, paper, and pencil.

   A. Measure the length of your chain of findings.

   Using the necessary pliers, attach your findings from left to right:

   - Option one: end cap #1 + clasp + ring + end cap #2

   - Option two: end cap #1 + ring #1 + clasp + ring #2 + end cap #2

   Then measure the length of your chain of findings from the tip of one end cap's barrel to the tip of the other's barrel, also to the nearest ⅛ᵗʰ".

Figure 7.1: A one-inch (1") chain of findings.

B. Decide upon the amount of play (sliding motion) you want between the bracelet and the wearer's wrist. For a lobster clasp, it is usually ¾"-1".

C. Do the math.

- Sample one: If your chain of findings is 1" long, your wrist measures 6" around, and you prefer 1" of play, you can cut your braid at 6" and end up with a 7" bracelet. This gives you 1" of play because your chain of findings equals your preferred length of play.

- Sample two: If your chain of findings is 1" long, your wrist measures 6" around, and you prefer ¾" of play, your chain of findings is longer than your play. You can either subtract ¼" from the 6" braid cut above or work backward to solve the problem a different way:

  6" wrist + ¾" of preferred play = 6¾"; and 6¾" – 1" chain of findings = a 5¾" braid.

- Sample three: You can split the difference between 6" and 5¾" with a 5⅞" cut. In other words, there is a little wiggle room in braid-cutting.

Warning: Do not cut your braid until reading Steps 3 and 4 first.

3. <u>Mark your braid for gluing and cutting</u>. Needed: braid, two twist ties, a ruler or measuring tape, and scissors. Cut the two twist ties in half to create four mini-ties which are referred to as #3-6 in Figure 7.2.

For simplicity's sake, let us assume that you selected the 6" cut in the step above and have tightly twist-tied the beginning and end of the useable section of your braid. (In Figure 7.2 twist ties #1 and #2 are shown in brown.)

- Next, twist-tie #3 (shown in green) a ½" below twist tie #1 (brown).

- From the middle of the braid between twist ties #1 and #3, measure off the 6" of braid needed for the bracelet. Mark that length with twist tie #4. (The reason #4 is missing in Figure 7.2 will be revealed in the next step.)

- Twist-tie #5 (shown in green) a ¼" above #4 (missing). Twist-tie #6 (shown in brown) a ¼" below #4 (missing). When you are through, you no longer need tie #4 and can remove it.

- Recheck your measurements and the tightness of your twist ties. Readjust as necessary.

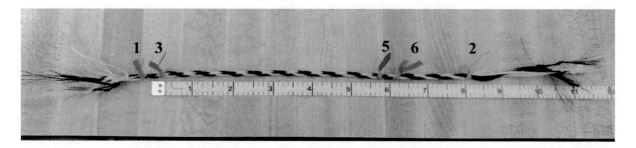

Figure. 7.2: A tied-off 8-string round braid shown in the black and white spiral pattern.

4. <u>The first gluing</u>. Needed: braid, newspaper, glue, and two toothpicks.

Do this step outdoors or in a well-ventilated room to reduce the amount of fumes that you inhale. Use newspaper to protect your work surface and make for easy cleanup. Lay out your glue and your toothpicks.

Very carefully (spilled glue is hard to remove, especially from your skin and findings), slowly and carefully rotate your braid as you apply glue between ties #1 and #3. (See Figure 7.3). Use a toothpick to spread the glue evenly over the entire area. Do not be skimpy with your glue but do not be overly generous either. Practice will help you learn just how much glue is needed.

Without allowing the glue to spread "outside the lines," reposition your grip. Apply glue on the braid between ties #5 and #6. Spread the glue over the entire area with the opposite end of your toothpick.

Figure. 7.3: Gluing between the ties.

Carefully loop your glued braid over a file drawer handle, a rung of a wooden chair, etc., to dry for a bit. If you are indoors, open a window or turn on a fan and leave the room to avoid breathing the fumes.

5. <u>Cut your braid and glue it into the end caps.</u> Needed: braid, chain of findings, scissors, glue, and clean toothpicks.

When you return to your workplace (which will depend on the glue you use and the stage of drying you prefer), remove both end caps from your chain of findings.

Carefully cut your braid evenly between ties #1 and #3. Quickly glue the newly exposed end. (If the container of your glue allows, you might dip the end of the braid into it.) Should the horsehair strings flare out, twist your toothpick and return them to braid diameter as you roll glue around the exposed end. (Picture the earth rotating as it revolves around the sun.) Reinforce the glue on the sides if necessary.

Repeat the process between ties #5 and #6. If you are lucky, the piece of braid you just cut off will be long enough for a second bracelet. If it is, check to see that tie #6 is secure.

Figure 7.4: A glued and cut braid.

Insert one braid end into end cap #1. Twist and push it in until it is flush with the tip of the barrel. Next, attach end cap #2 to the opposite end of the braid. Then carefully reattach the findings that fit in between the two end caps.

6. <u>Check the fit and lay of your bracelet.</u>

- The fit. If your wrist measurement is equal to or smaller than the bracelet you are making—and your glue has set enough to prevent your braid from pulling out of its end caps—try the bracelet on for size. If the bracelet is too small to try on, roll a cloth or face towel to the size of the wearer's wrist and fasten the bracelet round it.

  If the bracelet has only one ring and is slightly too short for the wearer's wrist, add a second ring at the opposite end of your chain of findings. If the bracelet is still too short, either add the proper gauge and length of jewelry chain to the findings or make a new braid.

  Conversely, when a bracelet with two rings is slightly too long, remove one of the rings and try to readjust the lay of your chain of findings. If the bracelet is still too long, try cutting it down and reapplying a salvaged end cap.

- The lay. This is especially important for the 6-string bracelet because of its flat side. If a bracelet does not lay flat against your wrist or on the table, check the vertical-horizontal orientation of the links in your chain of findings. If rotating an end cap does not solve the problem, you most likely made a braiding error that is impossible to fix at this point. Believe me, I have wasted hours trying!

  If the erroneous twist in the bracelet does not bother you, continue with the next step. If your error bothers you, chalk it up to experience and start a new braid. Making mistakes, learning from them, and being patient with yourself are important parts of the learning process.

  Make any other needed length or orientation adjustments before the glue completely sets. Add more glue if necessary.

7. <u>Crimp your end caps</u>. Needed: your needle-nose pliers.

   Check your gluing. Gently tug one end of the braid at the base of its end cap. Then gently tug the braid at the other end. If an end pulls out, it needs more glue and the glue needs to at least partially dry before you crimp.

   Review the three types of end caps in Figure 6.1. All have crimps: the ones for the 4- and 8-string braids are similar while the ones for the 4-string braid are quite different.

   Crimping the 4-string bracelet. Notice that the top coil of the end cap angles outward and is not closed all the way. With a pair of pliers, extend the coil until it is perpendicular to the rest of the coils. Then gently close the top coil into a ring. The bottom coil is the crimp. With your pliers, carefully pinch it against the braid.

   Crimping the 6- and 8-string braids. Extend your needle nose-pliers completely across the crimp, the middle of the end cap's three sections. Start crimping with gentle pressure, first in one direction across the braid and then in the other. Repeat with stronger pressure until you are satisfied with the tightness of your crimp. (I once broke a crimp by extending my pliers only halfway across it and crimping too hard the first time.)

8. <u>Final inspection (one to two full days after gluing the end caps)</u>. Needed: toothpick, tools, rubbing alcohol, a piece of cotton cloth (e.g., a handkerchief or bandana), and a clean toothbrush. Optional: a magnifying glass and a pair of tweezers.

   Recheck the security of your end caps again. If they are secure, use your magnifying glass to check for excess glue where none should be—below the base of the end caps, elsewhere on the braid, and/or on the findings. Use toothpicks to poke the excess glue under the end caps back up into them. A toothpick or pair of tweezers can also snag and pull or twist off any threads of glue on your braid. I often use my fingernails to scrape dry glue off of findings.

   Once all the excess glue is gone, clean your bracelet one last time. Gently wipe the braid and the findings with a cotton handkerchief or bandana soaked in rubbing alcohol.

   Because the glue that I use takes two days to completely dry, I do not wear my bracelets until then.

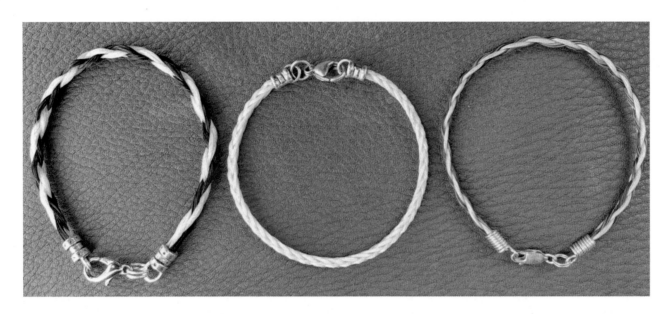

Figure 7.5: From left to right: a black and white easy 8-string round braid in the spiral pattern, a 6-string half-round braid in cream, and a red and white 4-string round braid in the striped pattern.

Chapter Eight
Caring for Your Bracelet(s)

Because horsehair bracelets are braided and glued into end caps, soaking them risks weakening the adhesive. This is why I appreciate the supporting role that crimps play in securing end caps.

If your horsehair bracelet gets dirty, gently clean it with a wet wipe or a cotton cloth or a soft-bristled toothbrush dipped into water or rubbing alcohol.

If a hair should bow out of your braid, try unfastening the bracelet and running a thumb and forefinger up and down the braid to push the bow back inside.

If the bow refuses, pull each end out a little farther. Carefully cut off each end with a nail clipper or a pair of manicure scissors. Upon release each cut end should disappear back into the braid.

Likewise, if an individual strand of horsehair should catch on something, break, and poke out from the braid, pull the offending hair a bit farther out and snip it off. Its remaining end should also disappear back into the braid.

Potential causes of bracelet separation include loose braiding, inadequate gluing, wearing before the glue is dry, and immersion into water for too long. With practice, you will become more adept at avoiding some of these problems.

Storing your bracelets in a tarnish free bag will keep the findings shiny longer.

Congratulations on working your way this far through the book. If you are looking for more challenges, the next chapter will keep you quite busy!

CHAPTER NINE
EXTENDING YOUR SKILLS

If you want to learn more, have a go at some of the challenges below.

1. Experiment with color patterns. D=dark (e.g., black or dark brown hair); M=medium (e.g., red, grey, or light brown hair); and L=light (e.g., yellow or white hair).

   - 4-string round braid: DDLL, DLDL, DDDL, and four different colors.

   - 8-string easy-round braid: DDDDLLLL, DDLLDDLL, and four different colors.

   - 6-string half-round braid: DDMMLL, DDDDMM, and DDDDDD.

   - Other color patterns of your own invention.

2. Mix black and white hairs together to create various shades of gray.

3. Use a jump ring or a split ring to add a charm to a bracelet.

4. If your horsehair is long enough, braid a necklace. Add a pendant with a hinged necklace enhancer (also known as a bale or a bail).

5. Research and learn some new braiding patterns.

6. List all the items created from horsehair throughout human history that you can discover.

7. Check out *Braiding with Horsehair* by Diane Gadway and Richard Schneider, 1984, for advanced braiding projects.

8. Look into hitching, a craft that combines hand-weaving and macramèing horse hair around a wooden dowel. When the dowel is completely encased, the horsehair "skin" (often with a geometric pattern) is slipped off and pressed flat into a belt or hatband. Three guides are:

   - *How to Hitch Horsehair* by Clay Christensen, 1992.

   - *Hitched Horsehair: The Complete Guide for Learning* by Shoni Maulding, 1997.

   - *Hitched Horsehair II: Advanced Patterns and Inlay Projects* by Shone and Ron Maulding, 2004.

Figure 9.1: Hitching around a leather browband. Photograph by Donna Murray.
Notice her table vise.

EPILOG

INTERTWINED AND EMBELLISHED
HEART STRINGS

I hope that this slightly edited version of Chapter 52 from my memoir, At Home on a Horse in the Woods: A Journey into Living Your Ultimate Dream (2019), helps to bring the fiber art of horsehair braiding alive for you.

I started Swishtails Custom Horsehair Jewelry in 2013, with the goal of creating keepsakes for clients bonded to their horses. In preparation for Derby 2015, Delanor, a Louisville jewelry designer, commissioned some short braids for her new earring concept. I made several sets of braids of various colors and patterns with an assortment of end caps. When I saw how Delanor incorporated my braids into her design, I wanted a custom pair to commemorate three special geldings.

The earrings had to be of my favorite braid, an 8-string round pattern difficult to make with horsehair. Years ago, before learning to braid, I had seen it on a horsehair braider's website, but, to my knowledge, neither of my two eventual teachers knew the pattern. Ultimately, I discovered it on YouTube. Long weeks of practice followed—first with parachute cord to learn the fingering, and then applying the fingering to strings of thinner, slicker, and less cooperative horsehair. Selecting the colors for the spirals in my earrings was easy—Dancer's white hair and Highlander's red. The execution, however, was more difficult.

Because mane hair is fine and short, tail hair is usually used for jewelry. I wanted pure red, the color of Highlander's mane and body, for the braid, but his tail hair is a mix of red, black, white, and clear—sometimes in a single strand! I could either harvest and sort through a lot of multi-colored ones in search of enough all-red ones or cut off just the amount of needed mane hair. As the latter alternative allowed Highlander to retain his complete tail for swishing away parasitic and pain-causing insects, my choice was obvious.

The next challenge was Dancer's hair—white near the rump but yellowed near the ground. Because I had been taught that it is impossible to wash away the yellow, I was stuck with the uneven coloration. Fortunately, however, half the hairs in a braid are arranged from rump (where they are thicker) to ground (where they are thinner) and a half from the ground to the rump. This results in a braid of even width throughout its entire length. (If all the hairs were arranged in the same direction, the braid would taper like a carrot.)

The result of this hair arrangement, in Dancer's case, would be a continuous cream braid instead of a white one merging into yellow. Then, because the textures of Highlander's mane and Dancer's tail hair differed, I experimented to figure out the ratio of red mane hairs to white tail hairs necessary, not only to create equally wide twists but also to fit into the end caps.

Once the hairs were selected, balanced, twisted, and braided, I glued and crimped them into sterling silver end caps. It was then time for Delanor to add the sterling silver ear mounts and charms that she designed.

But, it did not feel right to me that the earrings, made to honor my three favorite horses, were only braided from the hair of two, as I had not saved any of Geronimo's hair. At first, because he had been red and white, I told myself to pretend that his hairs were incorporated into the braid. But I would always know that they were not and wanted Geronimo to have a distinct presence of his own.

Recalling that his eyes had not been brown like Dancer's and Highlander's, I asked Delanor to attach a blue bead to each braid. After consultation on the right shade, she added Swarovski crystals.

I love wearing my earrings. I enjoy looking at them in the mirror and telling people their story. No matter where I am, I immediately, with a single magical tug, conjure up precious moments of my three godsends—Geronimo, Dancer, and Highlander.

Post Script: Designing custom horsehair jewelry is not only a creative outlet that helps me to support Highlander, it is also a blessing. By serving clients, I hear wonderful tales about the beloved horses, people, and ponies in their lives.

Figure E.1: Horsehair earrings made by Delanor Manson and Janet Wolanin Alexander.
Photograph by Letha Cupp.

ABOUT THE AUTHOR

Photo by Letha Cupp.

Janet taught science for 30 years and lives with her husband James, a biology professor, and their rescue cats and dogs in Southern Indiana. Besides braiding horsehair jewelry she loves horses, trail riding, nature, and writing.

Her first book was *At Home on a Horse in the Woods*. Its 2017 subtitle (*A Memoir*) was changed to *A Journey into Living Your Ultimate Dream* upon republication two years later.

For more information about Janet's jewelry or books, visit swishtails.com. To share your horsehair braiding experience, feel free to email a message and/or a photo to swishtails@aol.com.

Reviews really help authors. Please leave one for the bookseller from which you purchased this book. Thank you and happy braiding!